For

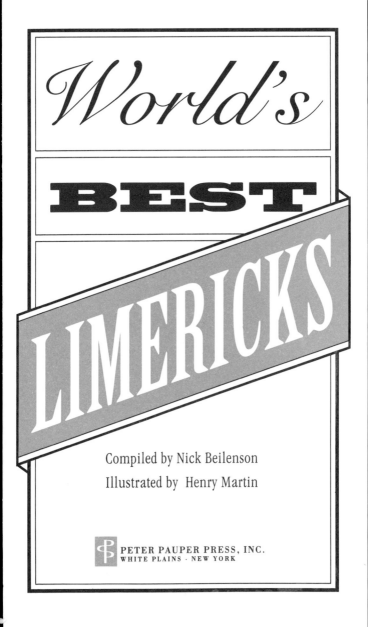

World's BEST LIMERICKS

Compiled by Nick Beilenson
Illustrated by Henry Martin

PETER PAUPER PRESS, INC.
WHITE PLAINS · NEW YORK

Dedicated to the memory of those we dared not print!

To The Reader

Peter Pauper Press first published limericks 40 years ago. Limericks weren't always clean then, even when they were "laundered," and they aren't always PG-13 now.

We at PPP take the high road—we print vulgar limericks but not obscene ones. Of course, where limericks are concerned, taste is a relative thing. So, turn off the cable TV, eject the videocassette, and prepare to be amused and perhaps even shocked.

We hope that this book will satisfy the "pent-up" demand for these 5-liners, and induce otherwise normal folk to try their hands at limericking.

The present collection draws on old chestnuts from the PPP files, and on new and topical limericks from members of The Limerick SIG (Box 365, Moffett, CA 94035), a Mensa Special Interest Group open to everyone. Our thanks to the Limerick SIG members who have permitted us to include their latest offerings.

N.B.

A cute little babe from St. Paul
Wore a newspaper dress to a ball;
    But the dress caught on fire
    And burned her entire
Front page, sporting section and all.

World's Best Limericks

There was a young maid from Madras,
Who had a magnificent ass;
     Not rounded and pink,
     As you probably think—
It was grey, had long ears, and ate grass.

❖ ❖ ❖ ❖ ❖

A cat in despondency sighed,
And resolved to commit suicide;
     She passed under the wheels
     Of eight automobiles,
And after the ninth one she died.

❖ ❖ ❖ ❖ ❖

Two elephants named Harry and Faye
Couldn't kiss with their trunks in the way.
     So they boarded a plane;
     Now they're kissing in Maine,
'Cause their trunks were sent on to L.A.

Irene D. Beavers

A shepherd was filled with concern
For a ram with great passion to burn,
      Until found, cold and stiff,
      At the foot of a cliff,
From failing to see a ewe turn.

                Robert F. Giandomenico

❀ ❀ ❀ ❀ ❀

There once was a maid with such graces,
That her curves cried aloud for embraces.
      "You look," said McGee,
      "Like a million to me—
Invested in all the right places!"

❀ ❀ ❀ ❀ ❀

An epicure, dining at Crewe,
Found quite a large mouse in his stew.
      Said the waiter, "Don't shout,
      And wave it about,
Or the rest will be wanting one, too!"

There was a young fellow named Willy
Who acted remarkably silly:
    At an All-Nations ball
    Dressed in nothing at all
He swore that his costume was Chile.

A smiling young lady of Niger,
Once went for a ride on a tiger;
>> They returned from the ride
>> With the lady inside,
And a smile on the face of the tiger.

❖ ❖ ❖ ❖ ❖

There was a young girl name Anheuser
Who said that no man could surprise her.
>> But Old Overholt
>> Gave her virtue a jolt,
And now she is sadder Budweiser.

❖ ❖ ❖ ❖ ❖

When the building contractor, O'Shea,
Saw his flooring begin to decay,
>> Enraged, he did utter,
>> "This stuff must be butter,
'Cause it sure as hell isn't parquet!"
>> *Loren C. Fitzhugh*

An optician once working in Delph,
Took his lens-grinder down from the shelf.
      He fell in (clumsy guy),
      In the blink of an eye,
Made a spectacle, there, of himself.

Robert F. Giandomenico

    ❀ ❀ ❀ ❀ ❀

There was a young lady named Kate,
Who necked in the dark with her date;
      When asked how she fared,
      She said she was scared,
But otherwise doing first-rate.

    ❀ ❀ ❀ ❀ ❀

A lunatic living at Lyme
Had honesty that was sublime;
      When we asked, "Are you there?"
      He said, "Yes, but take care,
For I'm never *all* there at one time."

There was a young warrior of Parma,
Who lovingly fondled his charmer.
    Said the maiden demure,
    "You'll excuse me, I'm sure,
But I wish you would take off your armor."

A maiden at college, named Breeze,
Weighted down by B.A.'s and M.D.'s
     Collapsed from the strain.
     Said her doctor, "It's plain
You are killing yourself by degrees!"

❖ ❖ ❖ ❖ ❖

I'd rather have fingers than toes;
I'd rather have ears than a nose;
     And as for my hair,
     I'm glad it's all there,
And I will be sad when it goes.

❖ ❖ ❖ ❖ ❖

Said a modest young fellow named Sam,
"I'm proud of how modest I am.
     I don't like to boast;
     Of my virtues—a host—
I'm as silent and close as a clam."

Laurence Perrine

God's plan made a hopeful beginning
But man spoiled his chances by sinning.
    We trust that the story
    Will end in God's glory;
But, at present, the other side's winning.

❀ ❀ ❀ ❀ ❀

There was a young driver named Jake
Who made the most stupid mistake:
    He drove through the wall
    And into the hall,
When he mixed up the gas and the brake.

❀ ❀ ❀ ❀ ❀

A dastardly brat from Bel Aire
Insists that he had an affair
    With his very own Mama—
    But she claims no trauma,
And says it was mostly hot heir.

Norm Storer

There was a young lady of Kent,
Whose nose was most awfully bent.
    One day, I suppose,
    She followed her nose,
And no one knows which way she went.

A desperate spinster from Clare
Once knelt in the moonlight all bare,
    And prayed on the sod
    To be taken by God
—But a passerby answered her prayer.

❀ ❀ ❀ ❀ ❀

No matter how grouchy you're feeling,
A smile is always quite healing;
    It grows like a wreath
    All around the front teeth.
Thus preserving the face from congealing.

❀ ❀ ❀ ❀ ❀

Said the Postmaster General, "Hooray!
I've something important to say:
    The letter you send
    From here to South Bend
Costs less than a penny a day."

Arthur J. Deex

Is there life after death?—I reply:
"You never will know till you die,
      And not then unless
      The answer is *Yes.*
If it's *No,* you won't know, nor care why."

                    Laurence Perrine

❀ ❀ ❀ ❀ ❀

There was a young housewife of Ayr,
Whose husband's homecomings were rare,
      Had he danced on her chest
      She'd have felt quite at rest,
For at least she'd have known he was there.

❀ ❀ ❀ ❀ ❀

There was an old fellow named Green,
Who grew so abnormally lean,
      And flat, and compressed,
      That his back squeezed his chest,
And sideways he couldn't be seen.

15

An accident really uncanny
Occurred to my elderly Granny;
      She sat down in a chair
        While her false teeth lay there,
And bit herself right in the fanny.

There were three little birds in a wood,
Who always sang hymns when they could;
     What the words were about
     They could never make out,
But they felt it was doing them good.

❈ ❈ ❈ ❈ ❈

There was a young man of Japan,
Who wrote verses that never would scan.
     When they said, "But the thing
     Doesn't go with a swing,"
He said, "Yes, but I always like to get as
many words into the last line as I
possibly can."

❈ ❈ ❈ ❈ ❈

A hot tempered biker named Dwight
Quite suddenly vanished from sight.
     Seems he was engaged
     In a quarrel, and enraged
He just flew off the handle one night.

Evelyn Bogen

A cheese that was aged and gray
Was walking and talking one day.
  Said the cheese, "Kindly note
  My mama was a goat
And I'm made out of curds by the whey."

❀ ❀ ❀ ❀ ❀

There was a young lady of Glasgow,
Whose party proved quite a fiasco.
  At nine-thirty, about,
  The lights all went out,
Through a lapse on the part of the Gas Co.

❀ ❀ ❀ ❀ ❀

Men once owned wives—bodies and wills.
They called all the shots, hogged the thrills.
  Now woman's been freed,
  Liberated indeed—
She is free to pay his and her bills.

Ann Gasser

18

An old maid in the land of Aloha
Got wrapped in the coils of a boa;
    And as the snake squeezed
    The maid, not displeased,
Cried, "Darling! I love it! Samoa!"

There was a young fellow of Perth,
Who was born on the day of his birth.
He was married, they say,
On his wife's wedding-day,
And he died when he quitted the earth.

❀ ❀ ❀ ❀ ❀

There was a young woman named Bright,
Whose speed was much faster than light.
She set out one day,
In a relative way,
And returned on the previous night.

❀ ❀ ❀ ❀ ❀

A chemistry student, named Chester,
Spent hours in lab each semester.
He discovered one week
A synthetic unique,
Which he named for his wife, Poly Esther.

Hobart H. Hatch

Have you heard of the Marlboro Man?
He's long, lean and rangy and tan;
      He puffs on the weed
      Up there on his steed
'Cause he can't in the family sedan.

Norm Storer

❀ ❀ ❀ ❀ ❀

There was a young poet of Kew,
Who failed to emerge into view.
      So he said, "I'll dispense
      With rhyme, meter, and sense,"
And he did, and he's now in "Who's Who."

❀ ❀ ❀ ❀ ❀

A golfer who came from Calcutta,
Had thoughts much too pungent to utter
      When his wife, as he found
      Ere commencing a round,
Was whisking the eggs with his putter.

A buxom young beauty named Beulah
Each night entertained with a hula;
    'Twas rather *risqué*
    In a mild sort of way,
But she made quite a bundle of moula.

A Tory, once out in his motor,
Ran over a Laborite voter.
        "Thank goodness," he cried,
        "He was on the wrong side,
So I don't blame myself one iota."

❧ ❧ ❧ ❧ ❧

A young man whose fad was pajamas,
Wore a suit of wool from the llamas;
        The unmanly effect
        Made people suspect
That the outfit was really his mama's.

❧ ❧ ❧ ❧ ❧

While strolling in Mayfair, I found
A young hook, so I said, "Fool around?"
        She said, "No hanky-panky.
        No sex with a Yankee.
The dollar's too weak v. the pound."

Theo M. Heller

Said the Madam, "You want Annie Tillett?"
Said the John, "That's my order, please fill it.
　　She's the lowest of tramps
　　But she gives me Green Stamps,
And my wife says she needs a new skillet."
Theo M. Heller

❀ ❀ ❀ ❀ ❀

A certain young laddie named Robbie
Rode his steed back and forth in the lobby;
　　When they told him, "Indoors
　　Is no place for a horse,"
He replied, "Well, you see, it's my hobby."

❀ ❀ ❀ ❀ ❀

When surprised by some callers from town
A housewife called down with a frown:
　　"In a minute or less
　　I'll slip on a dress"—
But she slipped on a rug and came down.

A clergyman told from his text
How Samson was scissored and vexed;
    Then a barber arose
    From his sweet Sunday doze,
Got rattled, and shouted, "Who's next?"

Mrs. Bobbitt

Let her name be preserved under lacquer.
When her husband presumed to attack her,
    An over-achiever,
    She reached for a cleaver
And proceeded to whack off his whacker.

Laurence Perrine

❁ ❁ ❁ ❁ ❁

There was a young man with a hernia,
Who said to his surgeon, "Gol dern ya,
    Now don't make a botch
    Of this job on my crotch,
Or cut things that do not concern ya."

❁ ❁ ❁ ❁ ❁

A husband who lived in Tiberias,
Once laughed himself nearly delirious;
    But he laughed at his wife
    Who took a sharp knife
With results that were quite deleterious.*

*With apologies to John Wayne Bobbitt

There was a young lady of Venice,
Who used hard-boiled eggs to play tennis.
When they said, "It is wrong,"
She replied, "Go along;
You don't know how prolific my hen is."

❀ ❀ ❀ ❀ ❀

A delighted incredulous bride
Remarked to the groom at her side:
I never could quite
Believe, till tonight,
Our anatomies *would* coincide.

❀ ❀ ❀ ❀ ❀

Loch Ness, nearly all will agree,
Is the scene of a deep mystery.
Does a sea-monster lurk
In the dark and the murk?
Who knows? It's a loch with no quay.

Laurence Perrine

A gorgeous voluptuous creature
Seduced a young Methodist preacher;
  It worked out quite well,
  For under his spell
This gal's now a Sunday-school teacher.

There once was a lusty Lothario
Who bedded twin blondes in Ontario;
  He said, "I'll confess,
  It was not without stress—
But sex is so *sexy* in stereo!"

        Norm Storer

❧ ❧ ❧ ❧ ❧

At the Zoo I remarked to an emu,
"I cannot pretend I esteem you.
  You're a greedy old bird,
  And your walk is absurd,
But your curious feathers redeem you."

❧ ❧ ❧ ❧ ❧

Gussie Bloom, while visiting Rome,
Went at Easter to see Peter's dome;
  She waved to the Pontiff
  A friendly "Good Yontiff!"
—"And Pope Paul waved back!" she wrote
home.

A young lady that folks thought was nice
Misbehaved with a man once or twice.
>
> She was married in May,
> In a family way,

And the guests at the church threw puffed rice.

Robert F. Giandomenico

❀ ❀ ❀ ❀ ❀

There was an old party of Lyme,
Who lived with three wives at one time.
>
> When asked, "Why the third?"
> He replied, "*One's* absurd,

And bigamy, sir, is a crime!"

❀ ❀ ❀ ❀ ❀

A dentist whose surname was Moss,
Fell in love with the charming Miss Ross;
>
> But he held in abhorrence
> Her Christian name Florence

So he called her his dear Dental Floss.

There was a kind curate of Kew,
Who kept a large cat in a pew;
     There he taught it each week
     A new letter of Greek,
But it never got further than Mu.

At a diplomat's ball in Rabat
Rabin said, "Arafat knows where it's at."
      DeKlerk said, "Mandela's
      A really swell fella."
Then all four of them got in a spat.

Thomas G. Keller

❀ ❀ ❀ ❀ ❀

There was a young lady of Wantage
Of whom the Town Clerk took advantage.
      Said the County Surveyor,
      "Of course you must pay her;
You've altered the line of her frontage."

❀ ❀ ❀ ❀ ❀

There was a young fellow from Tyne
Put his head on the South-Eastern line;
      But he died of ennui,
      For the 5:53
Didn't come till a quarter-past nine.

There was a young lady named Rood,
Who was such an absolute prude
That she pulled down the blind
When changing her mind,
Lest a curious eye should intrude.

❈ ❈ ❈ ❈ ❈

There once was a pious young priest
Who lived almost wholly on yeast;
"For," he said, "it is plain
We must all rise again,
And I want to get started, at least."

❈ ❈ ❈ ❈ ❈

Of all the world's verses recorded,
We find those most zealously hoarded
Are the limericks spun,
Which may prove that the pun
Is mightier, by far, than the sordid.

Robert F. Giandomenico

There was a young lady from Thrace
Whose corsets grew too tight to lace.
Her mother said, "Nelly,
There's more in your belly
Than ever went in through your face!'

There was a young fellow named Sydney,
Who drank till he ruined his kidney.
     It shriveled and shrank,
     As he sat there and drank,
But he'd had a good time at it, didn't he?

❈ ❈ ❈ ❈ ❈

There was a young lady of Lynn,
Who was so uncommonly thin
     That when she essayed
     To drink lemonade
She slipped through the straw and fell in.

❈ ❈ ❈ ❈ ❈

When making a cross-country hike,
I stick to the overland pike;
     I never use rivers—
     They give me the shivers,
For my barque is much worse than my bike.

Norm Storer

There was an old lady who said
When she found a thief under the bed,
    "So near to the door
    And so close to the floor,
I fear you'll take cold in the head."

❖ ❖ ❖ ❖ ❖

A limerick packs laughs anatomical
Into space that is quite economical.
    But the good ones I've seen,
    So seldom are clean,
And the clean ones so seldom are comical.

❖ ❖ ❖ ❖ ❖

Pray tell me if you should know
The name of the man, friend or foe,
    Believer or scoffer,
    Who last saw Jimmy Hoffa.
The answer's, of course, Jacques Cousteau.

Arthur J. Deex

A certain old maid of Cohoes,
In despair, taught her bird to propose;
    But the parrot, dejected
    At being accepted,
Spoke some words too profane to disclose.

"Dear Abby, my problem is I
Have a boyfriend—a wonderful guy.
     What gift should I seek
     For his birthday next week?"
"Never mind what he'd like . . . Give a tie!"

Arthur J. Deex

❀ ❀ ❀ ❀ ❀

God's plan made a hopeful beginning
But man spoiled his chances by sinning.
     We trust that the story
     Will end in God's glory,
But, at present, the other side's winning.

❀ ❀ ❀ ❀ ❀

There was a young girl named Bianca,
Who slept while the sloop was at anchor;
     But awoke, with dismay,
     When she heard the mate say:
"We must pull up the topsheet and spanker."

An indolent vicar of Bray
Let his lovely red roses decay;
        His wife, more alert,
        Bought a powerful squirt,
And said to her spouse, "Let us spray."

❄ ❄ ❄ ❄ ❄

A corpulent girl from Woods Hole
Had a notion exceedingly droll:
        At a masquerade ball,
        Dressed in nothing at all,
She backed in as a Parker House roll.

❄ ❄ ❄ ❄ ❄

The doctor informed Mr. Meek
That his wife needed sex twice a week.
        "If it's all right with her"
        Replied Mr. Meek, "I concur,
Do you think she would mind if I peek?"

Robert F. Giandomenico

There once was a corpulent carp,
Who wanted to play on the harp;
But to his chagrin
So short was his fin,
He couldn't reach up to C sharp.

A decrepit old gas man named Peter,
While hunting around for the meter,
      Scratched a match for a light,
      And rose up out of sight,
And, as anyone can see by reading this,
he also destroyed the meter.

❊ ❊ ❊ ❊ ❊

There was a young lady of Kent,
Who always said just what she meant;
      People said, "She's a dear—
      So unique—so sincere—"
But they shunned her by common consent.

❊ ❊ ❊ ❊ ❊

There was a young lady named Perkins,
Exceedingly fond of small gherkins.
      She went out to tea
      And ate forty-three,
Which pickled her internal workings.

I wish that my room had a floor;
I don't care very much for a door,
    But this walking around
    Without touching the ground
Is getting to be such a bore.

❧ ❧ ❧ ❧ ❧

There was a young maiden from Multerry,
Whose knowledge of life was desultory;
    She explained, like a sage:
    "Adolescence?—the stage
Between puberty and—er—adultery."

❧ ❧ ❧ ❧ ❧

One evening a hermit named Harry,
As he dined on some seeds and a berry,
    Said, "I would rather partake
    of a thick juicy steak
And perhaps a small glass of sherry."

Franklin L. Ward

A visitor once to Loch Ness
Met the monster, who left him a mess;
　　They returned his entrails
　　By the regular mails,
And the rest of the stuff by express.

I sat next to the Duchess at tea;
It was just as I feared it would be:
     Her rumblings abdominal
     Were simply phenomenal,
And everyone thought it was me!

❊ ❊ ❊ ❊ ❊ ❊

There was an old man in a hearse,
Who murmured "This might have been worse:
     Of course the expense
     Is simply immense,
But it doesn't come out of *my* purse."

❊ ❊ ❊ ❊ ❊ ❊

An amoeba named Sam, and his brother,
Were having a drink with each other;
     In the midst of their quaffing
     They split their sides laughing
And each of them now is a mother.

There was a young lady of Wilts,
Who walked to the Highlands on stilts.
When they said, "Oh, how shocking,
To show so much stocking,"
She answered, "Well, what about kilts?"

✿ ✿ ✿ ✿ ✿

There was a young lady of Kent,
Who said that she knew what it meant
When men asked her to dine,
And served cocktails and wine;
She knew, Oh she knew!—but she went!

✿ ✿ ✿ ✿ ✿

George Washington told the brigade
On the Delaware, "Men, I'm afraid,
Since advantage here lies
In total surprise,
The decision is row vs. wade."

A. N. Wilkins

A bather whose garments were strewed
On the beach where she sun-bathed all nude,
    Saw a man come along
       —And unless I'm quite wrong
You expected this line to be lewd.

There was an athletic young miss,
Who said, "Roller skating is bliss."
　　　This no more will she state,
　　　For a wheel off her skate
Made her finish up something like this.

❄ ❄ ❄ ❄ ❄

There was a young man so benighted,
He never knew when he was slighted.
　　　He went to a party,
　　　And ate just as hearty
As if he'd been really invited.

❄ ❄ ❄ ❄ ❄

There was a young lady of Erskine,
Who had a remarkably fair skin.
　　　When I said to her, "Mabel,
　　　You look well in your sable,"
She replied, "I look best in my bearskin."

A dentist who lives in Duluth
Has wedded a widow named Ruth,
      Who is so sentimental
      Concerning things dental
She calls her dear Second her Twoth.

❧ ❧ ❧ ❧ ❧

A young couple quite fond of croquet
Were ready one morning to play;
      But the grass was all wet
      So they said: "Better yet,
Let us play other games in the hay."

❧ ❧ ❧ ❧ ❧

Old Bill said, "We're gonna have N.A.F.T.A.
I'll buy it, by God, if I HAFTA!
      We'll get oodles and gobs
      Of good paying jobs—
Our constituents? They'll get the SHAFTA!"

Franklin L. Ward

An oyster from Kalamazoo
Confessed he was feeling quite blue,
    "For," he said, "as a rule,
      When the weather turns cool,
I invariably get in a stew!"

"When we build our new bathroom,"
said Fred,
"We will get a good blacksmith instead
    Of hiring a plumber,
    Who might take all summer.
This way we'll be forging a head."
Robert F. Giandomenico

❀ ❀ ❀ ❀ ❀

A fly and a flea in a flue
Were imprisoned, so what could they do?
    Said the fly, "Let us flee!"
    "Let us fly!" said the flea.
So they flew through a flaw in the flue.

❀ ❀ ❀ ❀ ❀

There was a young lady of Crewe
Who wanted to catch the 2:02.
    Said a porter, "Don't worry,
    Or hurry, or scurry,
It's a minute or two to 2:02."

On a bus at the end of the day
Miss Fifi was prompted to say:
      "Please give me your seat,
      I'm dead on my feet:
I'm with child—or at least *fatiguée.*"

❧ ❧ ❧ ❧ ❧

There once was a lady from Harris,
That not a thing seemed to embarrass
      Till the bath salts she shook
      In the tub that she took,
Turned out to be plaster of Paris.

❧ ❧ ❧ ❧ ❧

While I was departing the Prado,
I encountered a fierce desperado.
      As I went to surrender,
      A nearby fruit vendor
Knocked him out with a flung avocado.
Paul Lusch

There was a young man from Tacoma
Whose breath had a whiskey aroma;
    So to alter the smell
    He swallowed Chanel
And went off in a heavenly coma.

An old man to his doctor once fled,
"You must lower my sex drive," he said.
            "Give thanks you're so blessed,"
            Said the doctor, distressed.
"But it's all" said the man, "in my head!"
                    Robert F. Giandomenico

❖ ❖ ❖ ❖ ❖ ❖

There once was a fellow named Abbott
Who made love to girls as a habit;
            But he ran for the door
            When one girl asked for more,
And exclaimed "I'm a man, not a rabbit."

❖ ❖ ❖ ❖ ❖ ❖

You probably never have heard
Of this rather eccentric old beard,
            Who lived in a hole
            In the ground, the poor sole,
To get used to being inteard.

An erudite author was Holmes,
Who wrote some most ponderous tomes,
But somehow we feel
That their only appeal
Is to folks with protuberant domes.

❋ ❋ ❋ ❋ ❋

Said the Bishop one day to the Abbott,
Whose instincts were just like a rabbit:
"I know it's great fun
To embrace a young nun—
But you mustn't get into the habit."

❋ ❋ ❋ ❋ ❋

The rhinoceros rushing at Lorne
Made him wish he had never been born,
But Lorne held his ground
With his reason profound:
A dilemma with only one horn.

Albin Chaplin

An eccentric old person of Slough,
Who took all his meals with a cow,
　　Always said, "It's uncanny,
　　She's so like Aunt Fanny"—
But he never would indicate how.

There was a fat rabbit in Surrey
Who ran down the lane in a hurry;
       He remarked: "I'm pursued,
       And by God I'll be stewed
If I'm caught, and eaten with curry."

❃ ❃ ❃ ❃ ❃

Said the Duke to the Duchess of Avery,
"Forgive me for breaking your reverie;
       You've been sitting on *Punch*
       Since long before lunch—
Might I have it, before it's unsavory?"

❃ ❃ ❃ ❃ ❃

There once was a cow from St. Joe
Where green grass made her belch,
don't you know.
       But the bovine was plucky,
       Went off to Kentucky,
Ate blue grass. She mood indigo.

Don Moore

There was a young lady of Zion
Looked round for a shoulder to cry on;
    So she married a spouse
    From a very old house
And started to cry on the scion.

❋ ❋ ❋ ❋ ❋

There was an old spinster of Worcester
Who owned nine grey hens and a rooster;
    When the rooster expired
    She often inquired
Why there weren't new chicks like there uster.

❋ ❋ ❋ ❋ ❋

From the depths of a prison's confines,
Came a sad cocaine dealer's bleak whines,
    "How can limerists go free
    While a fellow like me
Gets busted for doing five lines?"

Robert F. Giandomenico

There was a fine lady of Herm,
Who tied bows on the tail of a worm;
      Said she, "You look festive,
      But don't become restive,
You'll wriggle 'em off if you squirm."

Pharaoh, a hard-working stork,
Was delivering a baby to York.
    He spilled its milk bottle,
    Had to shut down his throttle,
And feed it some cheese with a fork.

Nancy Henry Kline

❉ ❉ ❉ ❉ ❉

The limerick's an art form complex
Whose contents run chiefly to sex;
    It's famous for virgins
    And masculine urgin's,
And vulgar erotic effects.

❉ ❉ ❉ ❉ ❉

There was a tree surgeon named Dwight,
Who had an incredible fright.
    While curing a tree
    It alarmed him to see
That its bark was much worse than its blight!

Peggy S. Lewis

If intercourse gives you thrombosis
While continence causes neurosis,
        I prefer to expire
        Fulfilling desire
Than live on in a state of psychosis.

❀ ❀ ❀ ❀ ❀

There was a young woman named Sue
Who saw a strange beast in the zoo;
        When she asked, "Is it old?"
        She firmly was told,
"No! Certainly not! It is gnu."

❀ ❀ ❀ ❀ ❀

A dull-witted fellow once sped
To his doctor for pains in his head.
        His doctor said, "Jack,
        When you jump from the sack,
In the morning, try feet first instead."

Robert F. Giandomenico

There once was a sailor named Pink
Whose mates rushed him off to the clink.
      Said he: "I've a skunk
      As a pet in my bunk—
That's no reason for raising a stink."

A talented Greek was Achilles;
His prowess gave Trojans the willies;
    When the battle was spent,
    He would pitch his own tent—
Why, he could have played ball for the
Phillies!

          Norm Storer

❁ ❁ ❁ ❁ ❁

A brainy professor named Zed
Dreamed one night of a buxom co-ed;
    He mussed her and bussed her
    And otherwise fussed her,
But the action was all in his head.

❁ ❁ ❁ ❁ ❁

"My girl-friend wants me to ski,"
Said the flabby young cellist, "but Gee!
    With Stravinsky, Stokowski,
    Mussorgsky, Tchaikovsky,
That's quite enough skiing for me."

An amorous maiden antique
Locked a man in her house for a week;
    He entered her door
    With a shout and a roar,
But his exit was marked by a squeak.

❀ ❀ ❀ ❀ ❀

There was a young fellow from Clyde
Who fell down an outhouse and died;
    His unfortunate brother
    Then fell down another,
And now they're interred side by side.

❀ ❀ ❀ ❀ ❀

Said a researcher in nuclear fusion,
"My research will dispel all confusion,
    At least, it will later,
    After I've doctored my data
To make sure it supports my conclusion."
James M. Menger, Jr.

A plumber from Lowater Creek
Was called in by a dame with a leak;
      She looked so becoming
      He fixed *all* her plumbing
And didn't emerge for a week.

❖ ❖ ❖ ❖ ❖

In Summer he said she was fair,
In Autumn her charms were still there;
      But he said to his wife
      In the Winter of life
"There's no Spring in your old *derrière.*"

❖ ❖ ❖ ❖ ❖

The dinosaur no longer reigns
In the marshes or forests or plains.
      The beasts might have survived
      Where once they had thrived,
If only they'd grown bigger brains.

Paul Lusch